MY LOCKDOWN JOURNAL

Finding good memories in a year of madness.

To all the people wha have had to take 2020 one day at a time.

Just remember the good things that happened.

THESE MEMORIES BELONG TO

....

"It is not the strongest of the species that survive, nor the most intelligent, but the one most responsive to change."

Charles Darwin

WHY THIS BOOK?

The year 2020, what a year!

What started off as a virus that was on the other side of the world, soon turned into something none of us thought we would see in our lifetimes.

As the virus grew and became a pandemic, we were told as a country (England) to stay in, then eat out, meet people in a bar, but not in their gardens.

You could excercise once a day and toilet roll had the street value of gold (I actually saw a fight over a 9 pack of Charmin).

Schools were closed and people had to learn that home schooling was a nightmare whilst having to work from their kitchens.

This is a journal that I used to document memories with my family. I found that even though the world was going a little bit mental, a lot of good things happened too.

HOW TO USE THIS BOOK.

It's as simple as I could make it, it had to be for me!

Each "memory" is covered on two pages.

The first is where you can write, doodle, sketch, recall or whatever you want about a memorable thing. It may be a screen shot of a ZOOM quiz, it may be you dancing in your underwear in the sun, it's up to you.

The second page is for a photo, remember those? An actual photo, there are so many free apps there are no excuses.

That's it…now go!

YOUR MEMORIES
BEGIN HERE.

My memory title:

Date:

Location:

What is it?

Why is it memorable?

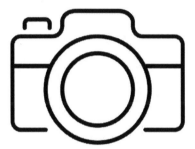

Pop your photo here

My memory title:

Date:

Location:

What is it?

Why is it memorable?

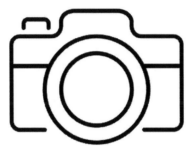

Pop your photo here

My memory title:

Date:

Location:

What is it?

Why is it memorable?

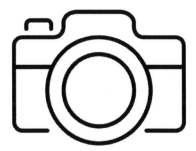

Pop your photo here

My memory title:

Date:

Location:

What is it?

Why is it memorable?

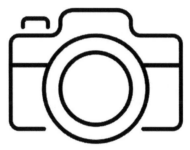

Pop your photo here

My memory title:

Date:

Location:

What is it?

Why is it memorable?

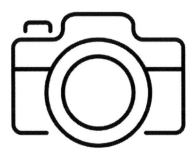

Pop your photo here

My memory title:

Date:

Location:

What is it?

Why is it memorable?

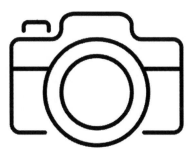

Pop your photo here

My memory title:

Date:

Location:

What is it?

Why is it memorable?

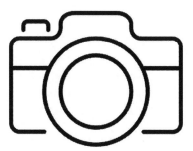

Pop your photo here

My memory title:

Date:

Location:

What is it?

Why is it memorable?

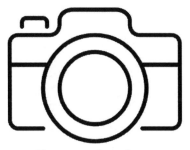

Pop your photo here

My memory title:

Date:

Location:

What is it?

Why is it memorable?

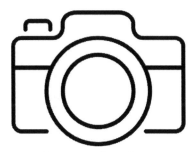

Pop your photo here

My memory title:

Date:

Location:

What is it?

Why is it memorable?

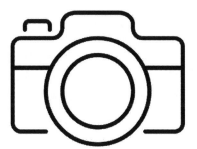

Pop your photo here

My memory title:

Date:

Location:

What is it?

Why is it memorable?

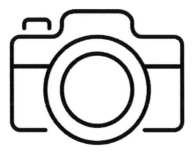

Pop your photo here

My memory title:

Date:

Location:

What is it?

Why is it memorable?

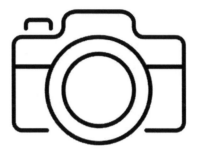

Pop your photo here

My memory title:

Date:

Location:

What is it?

Why is it memorable?

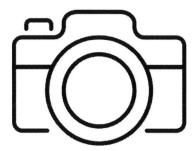

Pop your photo here

My memory title:

Date:

Location:

What is it?

Why is it memorable?

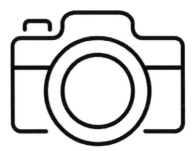

Pop your photo here

My memory title:

Date:

Location:

What is it?

Why is it memorable?

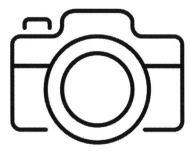

Pop your photo here

My memory title:

Date:

Location:

What is it?

Why is it memorable?

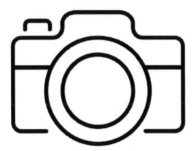

Pop your photo here

My memory title:

Date:

Location:

What is it?

Why is it memorable?

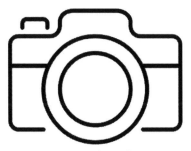

Pop your photo here

My memory title:

Date:

Location:

What is it?

Why is it memorable?

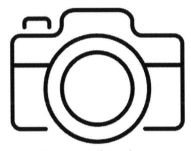

Pop your photo here

My memory title:

Date:

Location:

What is it?

Why is it memorable?

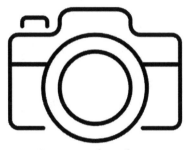

Pop your photo here

My memory title:

Date:

Location:

What is it?

Why is it memorable?

Pop your photo here

My memory title:

Date:

Location:

What is it?

Why is it memorable?

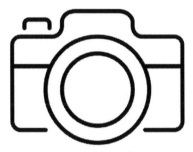

Pop your photo here

My memory title:

Date:

Location:

What is it?

Why is it memorable?

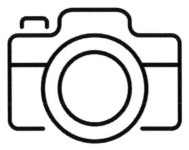

Pop your photo here

My memory title:

Date:

Location:

What is it?

Why is it memorable?

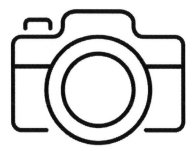

Pop your photo here

My memory title:

Date:

Location:

What is it?

Why is it memorable?

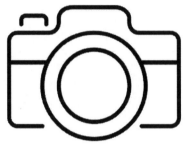

Pop your photo here

My memory title:

Date:

Location:

What is it?

Why is it memorable?

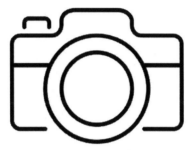

Pop your photo here

My memory title:

Date:

Location:

What is it?

Why is it memorable?

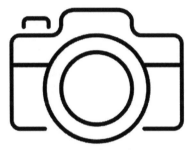

Pop your photo here

My memory title:

Date:

Location:

What is it?

Why is it memorable?

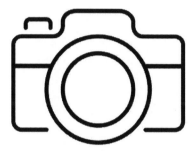

Pop your photo here

My memory title:

Date:

Location:

What is it?

Why is it memorable?

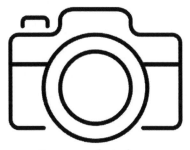

Pop your photo here

My memory title:

Date:

Location:

What is it?

Why is it memorable?

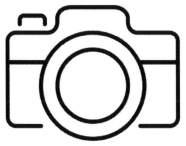

Pop your photo here

My memory title:

Date:

Location:

What is it?

Why is it memorable?

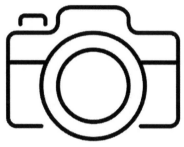

Pop your photo here

My memory title:

Date:

Location:

What is it?

Why is it memorable?

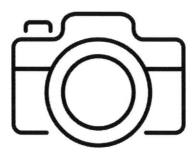

Pop your photo here

My memory title:

Date:

Location:

What is it?

Why is it memorable?

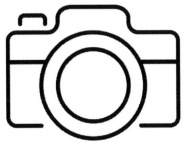

Pop your photo here

My memory title:

Date:

Location:

What is it?

Why is it memorable?

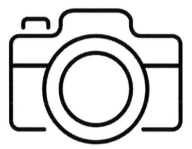

Pop your photo here

My memory title:

Date:

Location:

What is it?

Why is it memorable?

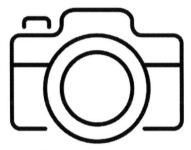

Pop your photo here

My memory title:

Date:

Location:

What is it?

Why is it memorable?

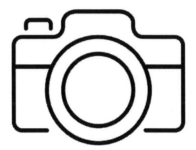

Pop your photo here

My memory title:

Date:

Location:

What is it?

Why is it memorable?

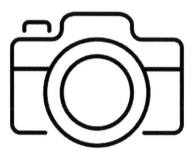

Pop your photo here

My memory title:

Date:

Location:

What is it?

Why is it memorable?

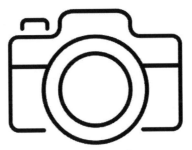

Pop your photo here

My memory title:

Date:

Location:

What is it?

Why is it memorable?

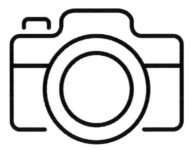

Pop your photo here

My memory title:

Date:

Location:

What is it?

Why is it memorable?

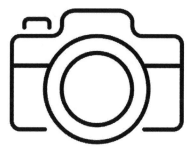

Pop your photo here

My memory title:

Date:

Location:

What is it?

Why is it memorable?

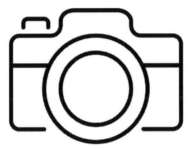

Pop your photo here

My memory title:

Date:

Location:

What is it?

Why is it memorable?

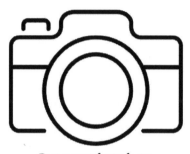

Pop your photo here

My memory title:

Date:

Location:

What is it?

Why is it memorable?

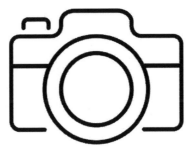

Pop your photo here

My memory title:

Date:

Location:

What is it?

Why is it memorable?

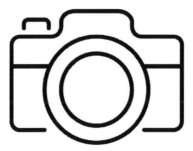

Pop your photo here

My memory title:

Date:

Location:

What is it?

Why is it memorable?

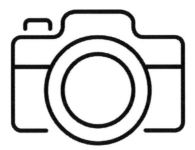

Pop your photo here

My memory title:

Date:

Location:

What is it?

Why is it memorable?

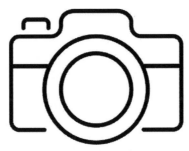

Pop your photo here

My memory title:

Date:

Location:

What is it?

Why is it memorable?

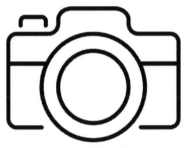

Pop your photo here

My memory title:

Date:

Location:

What is it?

Why is it memorable?

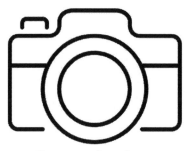

Pop your photo here

My memory title:

Date:

Location:

What is it?

Why is it memorable?

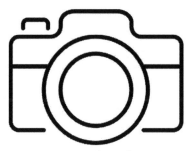

Pop your photo here

My memory title:

Date:

Location:

What is it?

Why is it memorable?

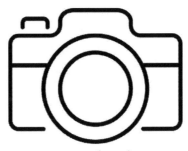

Pop your photo here

My memory title:

Date:

Location:

What is it?

Why is it memorable?

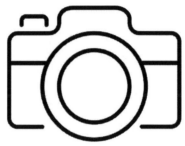

Pop your photo here

My memory title:

Date:

Location:

What is it?

Why is it memorable?

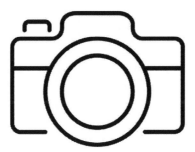

Pop your photo here

My memory title:

Date:

Location:

What is it?

Why is it memorable?

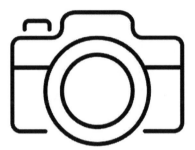

Pop your photo here

My memory title:

Date:

Location:

What is it?

Why is it memorable?

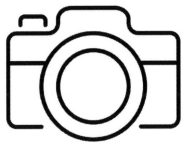

Pop your photo here

My memory title:

Date:

Location:

What is it?

Why is it memorable?

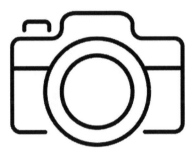

Pop your photo here

My memory title:

Date:

Location:

What is it?

Why is it memorable?

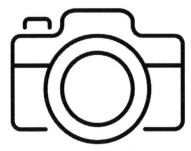

Pop your photo here

My memory title:

Date:

Location:

What is it?

Why is it memorable?

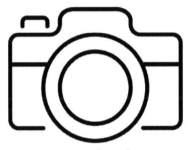

Pop your photo here

My memory title:

Date:

Location:

What is it?

Why is it memorable?

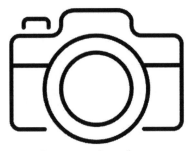

Pop your photo here

My memory title:

Date:

Location:

What is it?

Why is it memorable?

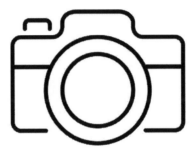

Pop your photo here

My memory title:

Date:

Location:

What is it?

Why is it memorable?

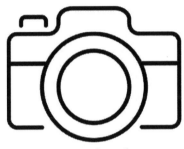

Pop your photo here

My memory title:

Date:

Location:

What is it?

Why is it memorable?

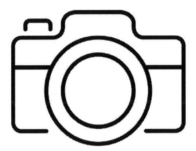

Pop your photo here

My memory title:

Date:

Location:

What is it?

Why is it memorable?

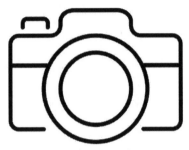

Pop your photo here

My memory title:

Date:

Location:

What is it?

Why is it memorable?

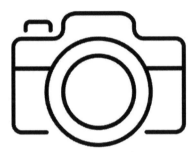

Pop your photo here

My memory title:

Date:

Location:

What is it?

Why is it memorable?

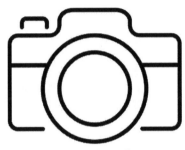

Pop your photo here

My memory title:

Date:

Location:

What is it?

Why is it memorable?

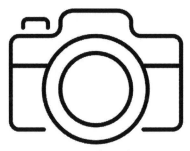

Pop your photo here

My memory title:

Date:

Location:

What is it?

Why is it memorable?

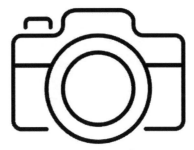

Pop your photo here

My memory title:

Date:

Location:

What is it?

Why is it memorable?

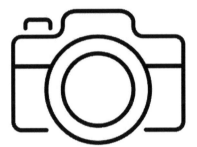

Pop your photo here

My memory title:

Date:

Location:

What is it?

Why is it memorable?

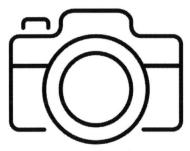

Pop your photo here

My memory title:

Date:

Location:

What is it?

Why is it memorable?

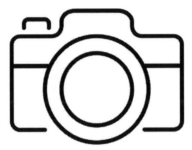

Pop your photo here

My memory title:

Date:

Location:

What is it?

Why is it memorable?

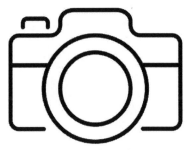

Pop your photo here

My memory title:

Date:

Location:

What is it?

Why is it memorable?

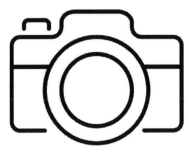

Pop your photo here

My memory title:

Date:

Location:

What is it?

Why is it memorable?

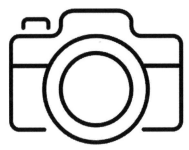

Pop your photo here

My memory title:

Date:

Location:

What is it?

Why is it memorable?

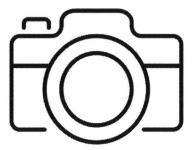

Pop your photo here

My memory title:

Date:

Location:

What is it?

Why is it memorable?

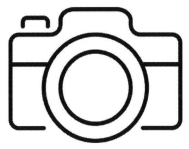

Pop your photo here

My memory title:

Date:

Location:

What is it?

Why is it memorable?

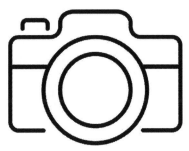

Pop your photo here

My memory title:

Date:

Location:

What is it?

Why is it memorable?

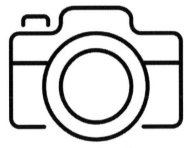

Pop your photo here

ENJOY WHAT YOU HAVE

I hope you got the satisfaction from completing and revisiting memories from the year in this journal.

For me, it made me realise that for all of the bad, there is also alot of good that happened.

As a generation, we have not seen anything like this before. It has brought out the best and worst in us as humans.

All you can do is make sure you enjoyed some of what happened.

✳ ✳ ✳

"I KNOW FOR SURE WHAT WE DWELL ON IS WHAT WE BECOME."

Oprah Winfrey

ABOUT THE AUTHOR

Andy Gumbley

Originally from Birmingham, Andy lives has lived in Bedfordshire since 2004. He now lives with his wife Charlotte, 2 children Oz and Aria, his dog Pepper and fish Conan

Previously a primary school teacher, Andy now owns a swim school back in Birmingham with his little but bigger brother, Matt.

During Lockdown in March, Andy decided to start putting his ideas on paper, originally in the form of a book that has a naughty word it (so we can't print it here).

During the second Lockdown, he created journals to document places he had been with his son Oz and daughter Aria.

Andy now writes under 3 different pseudonyms.

A.D Gumbley, where he documents the good, the bad and the ugly sides of life.

Andy Gumbley, where he creates journals and diaries to build memories of adventures and times spent with loved ones.

Sven Moon-Dragon where he writes books for children and young people.

Andy can be found on social media;
@dadventuretimes
@myramblingsinwriting

Printed in Great Britain
by Amazon